The Art of
CHRISTMAS
CRAFTS

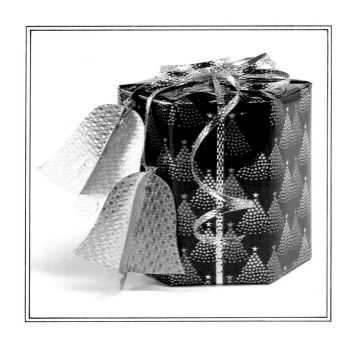

These miniature crackers can be hung on the Christmas tree or on the wall. First take a piece of cartridge (drawing) paper or light cardboard about 8cm (3in) wide and long enough to roll into a tube. Hold it together with a little sticky tape.

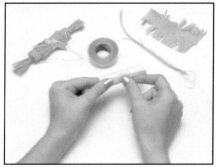

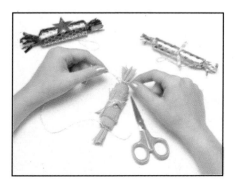

Cut a piece of crepe paper or foil twice as long as the tube, and roll the tube in it. Stick the edges together with double-sided tape. Squeeze the paper together at both ends, and tie some thread around them. Fluff out the ends and make small cuts in them to make a fringe.

To decorate the cracker, cut some extra, narrow pieces of crepe paper or foil, fringe them at the edges and wrap them around the tube as before. Alternatively, tie a bow round the cracker or stick a silver star in the middle. Tie a length of ribbon or sparkly twine to the ends by which to hang the cracker.

By the time Christmas arrives, you may not have much extra cash for Christmas tree baubles, so these colourful fakes are a great way of economizing. First cut some circles, with a little loop on the top, from some lightweight cardboard. Now mark out a pattern on each in pencil. Simple zigzags and curved lines are effective, but not too complicated to fill in.

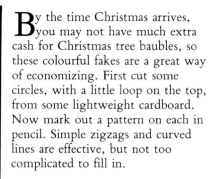

Paint each bauble with several different colours, waiting for each to dry before painting the next. If you have some gold or silver paint, make good use of this, as it is very effective. Use black to make definite lines between colours.

When the baubles are dry, attach some thread, ribbon or, as shown, some tinsel wire, so that you can hang them up.

If you haven't any shiny bells for the Christmas tree, it's not difficult to make some from foil, beads and a little string. First take a saucer and mark around it onto the back of some coloured foil. Cut out the circle, then fold it in half, and cut along the fold line. Fold each half of the circle into a cone and glue it in place.

These miniature lanterns make attractive Christmas tree ornaments. First take a piece of foil-covered paper 11cm (5½in) square. Fold it in half, and rule a line 1.5cm (¾in) from the loose edges. Now rule lines 1cm (½in) apart, from the fold up to this first line. Cut along these lines and open out the sheet of paper.

For the clapper, string a bead onto a length of thread — preferably waxed — and tie a knot over the bead. Lay the thread against the bell so that the clapper is at the right level, then tie a knot level with the hole in the top. This prevents the string from being pulled through the hole when threaded. Pull the string through the hole from the inside and thread on a smaller bead at the top; knot in place.

Hold the paper with the cuts running vertically, and glue the two sides together. When this is firm, set the lantern on the table and gently push the top down to make the sides poke outwards.

Finish each bell by dabbing a little glue around the bottom edge and sprinkling on some glitter. When you have made three bells, string them together, and attach them to a ring so that they can be hung on the tree. Wind a little tinsel wire around the string, and tie a couple of bows for that final touch of glamour.

Finally, cut a strip of matching paper 13cm (5in) long and 1cm (½in) wide. Dab some glue on each end, and glue the strip onto the inside of the lantern, at the top, for a handle.

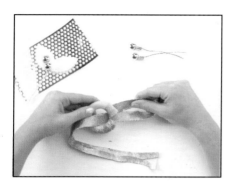

Add a touch of regal splendour to your tree with these golden decorations. To make a miniature wreath, first wind the wires of two silk leaves and two small glass balls together, and bind with white florist's tape. Cut a 16cm (6½in) length from sequin waste. Next cut a long strip of gold crepe paper, fold the edges in and bind around a small wooden ring.

Tie a loop of gold thread around the ring at the paper join. Twist the leaf and ball stems around the ring over the thread, folding in the wire ends to secure.

Fold the ends of the sequin waste into the centre so that they overlap, with the selvedges at each side. Thread a long length of fine florist's wire down the middle, through all the layers. Then thread the wire back and pull up gently to make a bow shape. Twist the wires tightly to secure and bind them around the leaf wires. Arrange the leaves, bow and balls attractively over the ring.

To make a jewelled sphere, first wrap a polystyrene ball with gold crepe paper: cut a square of paper to fit generously, and pull it up tightly over the ball. Tie firmly around the gathered paper with a length of gold thread, and knot the ends of the thread to make a hanging loop. Cut a strip of crepe paper to make a bow and fold the raw edges in. Pinch the strip into a bow shape.

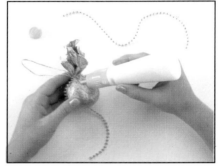

Run a line of clear adhesive around the ball and press a strip of beading trim into it. Repeat with a line of beading crossing in the opposite direction. Stick 'jewels' between the beads and large sequins, held in place with a pearl-headed pin. Trim the paper at the top of the sphere and attach the bow with a sequin trimmed pearl-headed pin.

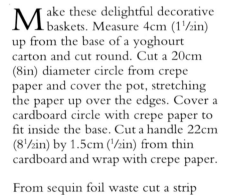

Make these delightful decorative baskets. Measure 4cm (1½in) up from the base of a yoghourt carton and cut round. Cut a 20cm (8in) diameter circle from crepe paper and cover the pot, stretching the paper up over the edges. Cover a cardboard circle with crepe paper to fit inside the base. Cut a handle 22cm (8½in) by 1.5cm (½in) from thin cardboard and wrap with crepe paper.

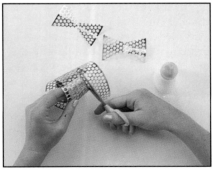

From sequin foil waste cut a strip long enough to wrap around the pot. Run a line of glue along the top and bottom of the pot and in one vertical line. Wrap the foil round, pressing into the glue, and trim, straightening the overlap along the vertical line of glue. Cut two strips 5cm (2in) wide from sequin waste, fold in half, selvedges level, and cut into bow shapes.

Staple the handle and foil bows each side of the basket. Tie bows from lengths of satin ribbon and stick over the foil bows with double-sided tape. Stick a pad in the bottom of the basket and arrange a bunch of glass baubles on top.

Here's an attractive way to add sparkle to the Christmas tree. You can buy these plain glass balls from craft suppliers, so look in craft magazines for stockists or try your nearest craft shop. As you are decorating a curved surface, it is advisable to keep the design simple. Draw the outlines of your design using a fine multi-purpose felt tip paint pen.

Try to place the motifs evenly, remembering you will see the far side of the design through the glass ball. Fill in the design with the same colour you used for the outlines. You can rub out any mistakes with a cloth soaked in turpentine.

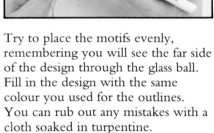

Outline your motifs in a contrasting colour, combining colours such as red and green, yellow and black, pink and purple. Add tiny dots between the motifs using the same colour as that used for the outline. Hang the baubles from your tree with gold gift wrapping thread.

BLUE ANGEL

CHRISTMAS STAR

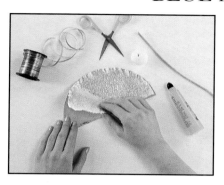

Cut a 10cm (4in) diameter semi-circle of silver cardboard, silver crepe paper and crinkly film. Trim the curve of the film in zig-zags and flute the crepe paper curve between your thumb and finger. Place the crepe paper on the cardboard with the film on top and glue together along the straight edges. Overlap the straight edges in a cone and glue.

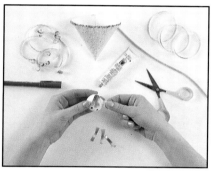

Draw eyes with a black pen on a 3.5cm (1½in) diameter cotton pulp ball. Cut short pieces of narrow giftwrap ribbon and glue to the head as a fringe. Cut longer pieces and pull the ends over a knife blade to curl them, then glue over the head. Glue ribbon around the head, then cut a slit in the base of the head and push the cone point through.

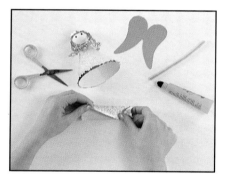

Cut silver crepe paper 11cm x 6cm (4½in x 2¼in) and flute the ends. Glue the long edges together and insert a 15cm (6in) pipecleaner for the arms through the tube and bend back the ends. Squeeze the centre and glue behind the cone, bending the arms forward. Use the template on page 163 to cut silver cardboard wings and glue them in place behind the angel.

From cartridge paper cut two rectangles, one 58cm by 10cm (23in x 4in), the other 58cm by 6.5cm (23in x 2½in). Mark each one into 12mm (½in) strips and draw a line 2.5cm (1in) from the long edge. Following your marks, cut out a zig-zag edge and pleat the strips. Use spray adhesive to stick gold foil to each side of the large rectangle, and silver foil to the smaller one.

Pleat the gold strip again and fold it into a circle. Join the two ends with double-sided tape and prevent the centre from popping up by smearing glue into the centre. Weight down the star with a book until it is dry. Next make a loop from gold thread from which to hang the star, and glue this to the centre of the star at the back.

Make up the silver star as before and place a double-sided adhesive pad on the centre back. Use this to attach the star to the gold star, aligning the pleats. Finally, put a little glue into the centre of the star and press a small glass ball in place.

Cover cotton craft ball with a double layer of nylon tights. The hole in ball should be at the neck. Cut a square of nylon and stretch over ball gathering at neck, sew through tights and bind with thread to form a neck. Trim nylon if necessary. Push neck into body gathers and sew through body and neck to secure head. Sew braid around body.

For the girl: Cut 20cm (8in) narrow lace. **For the clown:** Use the green ruff. Sew short edges together and gather one long edge. Place circle over head with join at the back, pull up tightly around neck and secure thread. Tie narrow ribbon around clown's neck with bow at front.

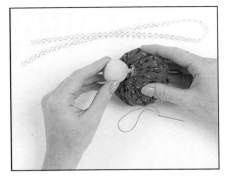

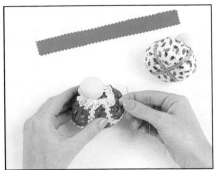

MATERIALS: *Printed cotton fabric; lining fabric; white or green fabric; decorative braids, narrow lace, narrow red ribbon; 1 × 25mm (1in) diameter cotton craft ball, 2 black map pins 1 flesh colour pipe cleaner for each doll; flesh colour nylon tights; matching sewing threads; tiny red pom poms or beads; 5cm (2in) diameter circle thin card; filling; red crayon; clear drying craft glue; pinking shears*

Press ½cm (¼in) to wrong side on all edges of sleeves. With wrong sides facing fold sleeve along centre length and slip stitch long edges together. Fold over 1.5cm (⅝in) at ends of pipe cleaner to make hands. Slip arms into sleeve, gather and sew fabric around wrists. Sew braid at wrists. Place arms around body with back under ruff and sew leaving front arms free.

For either doll: Cut body circle 18cm (7in) diameter and sleeves 13cm x 5cm (5in x 2in) in print fabric; inner body circle 18cm (7in) diameter in lining fabric; body base circle 5cm (2in) diameter in card.
For the girl: Cut hat circle 8cm (3in) diameter in white fabric. **For the clown:** Cut hat from print fabric; ruff 13cm x 2cm (5in x ¾in) in green using pinking shears.

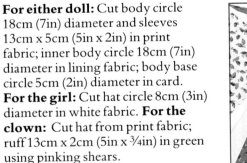

Sew lace around edge of right side of girl's hat. Sew running stitches 1.5cm (⅝in) from fabric edge to gather. Pull up stitches until hat fits head, add filling to crown and sew hat to head around gathers. Sew ribbon above gathers and tie with bow in front. Sew or glue pom pom or bead to centre of neck lace.

For either doll: Sew long running stitches around edge of inner body circle. Mould filling to make a ball of about 7.5cm (3in) diameter and place in centre of inner body. Pull up stitches to gather edge tightly and secure. Glue card base to cover stitches. Gather edge of body circle. Place card base to centre of wrong side of body. Pull up stitches.

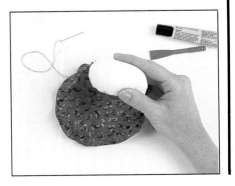

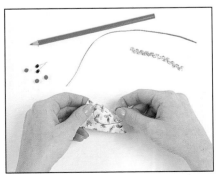

Sew clown's hat seam A–B. Turn to right side. Fill with stuffing and sew to head around edge. Sew braid to cover edge, sew or glue one pom pom or bead to front and three to body centre front. Glue back of map pins and press into head. Mark mouth in red crayon. Cut 20cm (8in) narrow ribbon, fold in centre, sew ends to body and loop to back of head to balance doll.

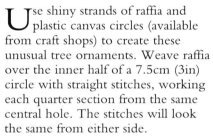

U̲se shiny strands of raffia and plastic canvas circles (available from craft shops) to create these unusual tree ornaments. Weave raffia over the inner half of a 7.5cm (3in) circle with straight stitches, working each quarter section from the same central hole. The stitches will look the same from either side.

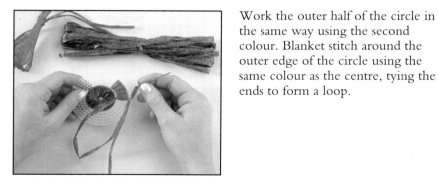

Work the outer half of the circle in the same way using the second colour. Blanket stitch around the outer edge of the circle using the same colour as the centre, tying the ends to form a loop.

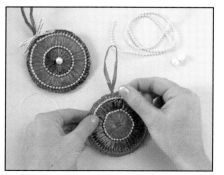

On each side, handsew pearl bead trim between the two halves of the straight stitches and around the outer edge. Sew a pearl button to the centre on each side. To finish, tie a silver ribbon bow around the base of the loop.

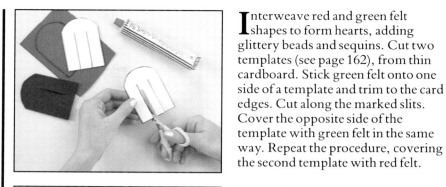

I̲nterweave red and green felt shapes to form hearts, adding glittery beads and sequins. Cut two templates (see page 162), from thin cardboard. Stick green felt onto one side of a template and trim to the card edges. Cut along the marked slits. Cover the opposite side of the template with green felt in the same way. Repeat the procedure, covering the second template with red felt.

Interlock the two shapes together by weaving the strips over and under their opposite number to form a heart shape.

Punch a hole centrally in the top of the heart; thread with a 20cm (8in) length of gold cord and tie into a loop. Finally, decorate each side of the heart with sequins and beads; either glue or handsew them in place.

Here is a lovely sparkly garland to hang at Christmastime. Cut Christmas tree and bell shapes from foil-covered cardboard, marking the shapes out first on the wrong side. Be careful when cutting as foil cardboard tends to crinkle at the edges.

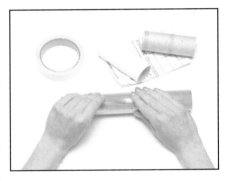

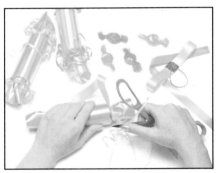

Make a tiny hole in the top of each, using a hole punch, or the tip of a skewer. Using red twine, tie each shape to a long strand of tinsel, leaving even spaces between them. At the top of each bell, fix a bow of gold-covered wire; on the trees, a little star.

The paper used for these crackers is similar in texture to curling gift wrap ribbon and has a lovely shiny satin finish. Cover empty toilet paper rolls or cardboard tubes with white sticky-backed plastic, which prevents the colour from showing through. Now cut pieces of shiny paper, twice as long as the tubes, and wide enough to go easily around them.

Wrap the tube in the paper and fix in place with double-sided tape. Don't twist the ends; scrunch them in with elastic (rubber) bands, which you can then cover with strips of curling ribbon. Decorate the crackers with boiled sweets (hard candies), stuck on with double-sided tape. Staple the crackers onto a strip of tinsel and trim the garland with sweets and baubles.

Alarge foil star to hang in the centre of the ceiling or over the fireplace. Try it out on a piece of ordinary paper first, as it is a little fiddly. Cut a piece of foil paper about 45cm (18in) square. Fold it in half from corner to corner, then in half twice again, making a small triangle.

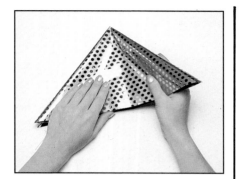

Bend the single-fold edge over to the edge with three folds. Open it out, and rule two lines from the corners at the base of the triangle to the centre crease. Cut along these two lines.

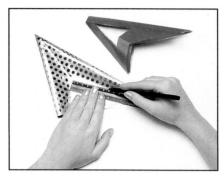

Refold the crease and rule two more lines, forming a small triangle as seen here. Cut this out. Now snip the point off and open the star out. Glue it to another piece of thicker foil paper for backing and cut the star out carefully when the glue has dried. Finish it off with a ribbon rosette in the centre.

You can always have snow at Christmas, even when the sun is shining outside. Make this snowflake in foil or in plain white paper and hang it over a window-pane. First take a square of paper, fold it into quarters, then in half diagonally, then lastly back on itself as shown.

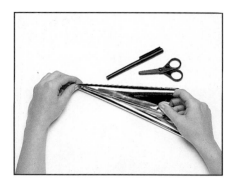

Make a pattern of the chosen design, then mark it on the folded paper with a black felt pen. Shade the areas that are to be cut away, then cut them out. Open out the snowflake. If you use a very flimsy foil, glue the snowflake onto a piece of paper, and cut out around it. This will make it easier to hang.

Finally, decorate the snowflake with sequins in bright jewel colours. The more patience you have, the more sequins you will use and the better it will look!

Make these shiny decorations from foil wrapping paper. Cut out eight circles in each of the following diameters: 9cm (3½in), 7.5cm (3in) and 6cm (2¼in). Then from cardboard cut out four circles 2cm (¾in) in diameter and two of 1.5cm (½in) for the centres. Fold the largest foil circles into quarters and staple four of them onto a large cardboard circle.

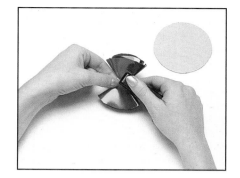

In the same way, staple the other four foil circles to another cardboard circle. Glue the two cardboard circles together with a string between them. Leave a long piece hanging below for the other two balls. Fluff out the edges of foil to make a good shape.

This simple star can be hung on the wall or from the ceiling. First make the pattern for the star. Using a ruler and protractor, draw an equilateral triangle (each angle is 60°). Cut out the triangle and use it as a pattern to make another one. Then glue one triangle over the other to form the star. Use this pattern to cut a star from foil paper.

Now make the other two balls in the same way, using the smaller cardboard circles for the tiniest. Fix the balls to the string as you go.

Fold the star in half three times between opposite points. Next fold it in half three times between opposite angles as shown. Every angle and point should now have a fold in it.

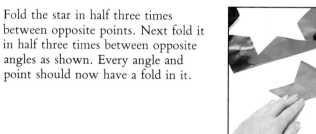

The star will now easily bend into its sculptured shape. Make a small hole in its top point with a hole punch or a skewer, then put some thread through the hole to hang it up.

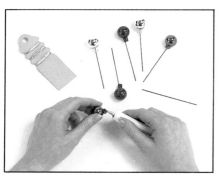

For a bright party centrepiece — ideal for Christmas or New Year's Eve — fill a glass bowl with a mixture of shiny glass baubles, foil crackers, feathers and streamers. To make clusters of small baubles, first remove the hanging string. Put a dab of glue inside the neck of each bauble and push in a short length of florist's wire. Leave them to dry.

Hold the wired baubles in a cluster and wind fine fuse wire around the stems to hold them together.

Wrap a piece of shiny giftwrap ribbon around the stems and tie it into a bow. Arrange the baubles and other ornaments in the bowl as shown.

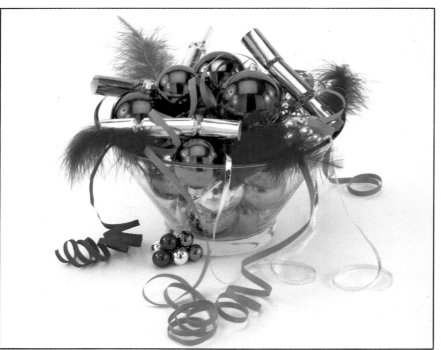

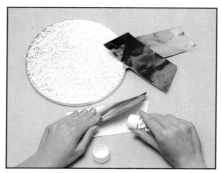

Believe it or not, this arrangement is quite simple once you get the hang of folding the cones. You need two colours of foil paper. Cut out lots of boat shapes 16.5cm (6½in) along the top and 12.5 (5in) along the bottom and about 6cm (2½in) deep. Glue one colour to another, back-to-back.

Form each boat into a cone and glue it in place. The first few you make may not look too professional, but it doesn't matter; these can go on the outside of the stand and will be partially covered. You will soon get the hang of folding the cones. Bend the bottoms under; it helps to hold the shape and looks tidier.

When you have several cones made, start gluing them around the edge of a 20cm- (8in-) diameter silver cake board. Place another two layers inside the first, leaving room for a chunky candle in the middle.

Gold and silver look stunning by candlelight and this festive arrangement will flatter any table setting. To begin, spray a vine garland with gold paint, sprinkle with gold glitter, and leave to dry.

Take three flat-based candle holders and stick florists' fixative putty under each one. Position them evenly around the garland, using florists' wire to secure each holder firmly in place.

To make the silver roses cut strips of silver crepe paper 53cm (21in) by 9cm (3½in). Fold in half lengthways and tuck the short ends in. Run double-sided tape along the lower edge of a folded strip and place a wired group of gold balls at one end. Roll the crepe paper around the balls, pinching the paper tightly together at the base. Finally, crimp the petal edges to curve outwards.

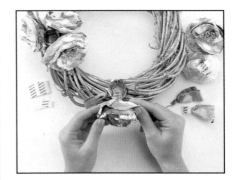

Stick a double-sided adhesive pad to the base of each rose and position four flowers around each candle holder. Cut 23cm (9in) lengths of gold ribbon and fold into double loops. Secure the ends with florists' wire and stick between the roses using adhesive pads. Tease the rose petals and gold loops to shape to hide the holders and put candles in place.

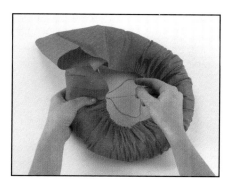

Adorn the New Year dinner table with this attractive centrepiece. Cut a length of crepe paper 120cm x 20cm (48in x 8in). Stick the ends together on the wrong side with clear sticky tape. Place a 25cm (10in) diameter polystyrene ring in the middle and sew the long edges of crepe paper together with a running stitch enclosing the polystyrene ring. Gather up the seam and fasten off.

Spray five candle holders white and push into the ring evenly spaced apart. Then drape strings of white pearls and narrow green coiled giftwrapping ribbon around the ring, gluing the ends to the underside.

Stick two rectangles of metallic blue cardboard back to back with spray adhesive and cut out five masks using the template on page 47. Score gently along the fold line of the tabs with a craft knife and bend the tabs backwards. Stick each mask by the tabs, in front of a candle.

Glue tiny blue and green star-shaped sequins to the ring, then cut out ten small stars from silver cardboard and glue between the candles and to each mask. Finally, place silver candles in the holders.

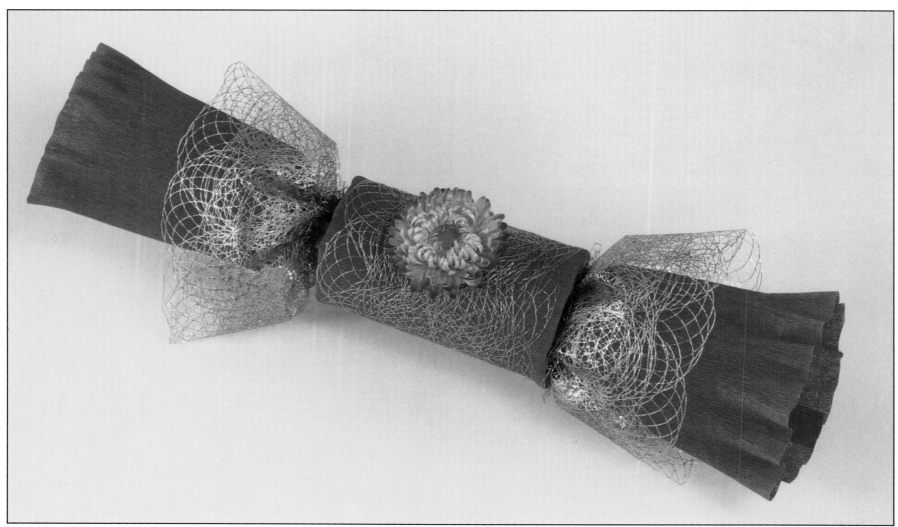

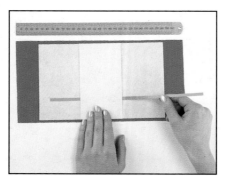

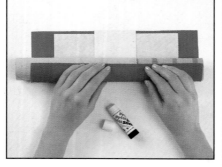

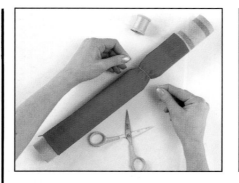

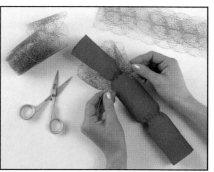

It is easy and economical to make crackers. Cut crepe paper 32cm x 16cm (12³⁄₄in x 6¹⁄₄in), keeping the grain of the paper parallel with the long sides. Lay a piece of thin writing paper 24cm x 15cm (9¹⁄₂in x 6in) centrally on top. Next cut thin cardboard 15cm x 8cm (6in x 3in) and lay it across the centre. Slip a cracker snap underneath.

Take two cardboard tubes, the sort found inside rolls of kitchen towel, and cut one in half. Lay the long tube on the lower edge of the crepe paper, with the end level with the cardboard edge. Butt a short tube against the long one and roll up tightly. Glue the overlapped edges of paper together with a low-tack adhesive.

Pull the short tube out for 5cm (2in) and tie thread tightly around the cracker between the tubes. Push the tubes together again then remove the short tube. Drop a gift, motto and paper hat inside and pull out the long tube a further 12.5cm (5in). Tie thread tightly between the tube and cardboard inside the cracker. Untie the threads.

Cut two 25cm (10in) lengths of gold filigree lace – the kind that has a drawstring thread along one edge. Gather up the drawstring and tie the lace around the necks of the cracker. Gently stretch the ends of the cracker to flute the edges. Remove the drawstring from a length of lace and glue around the middle of the cracker. Glue a dried flower to the cracker to complete.

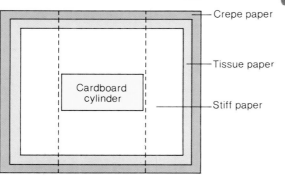

Crepe paper

Tissue paper

Cardboard cylinder

Stiff paper

Gather the paper together at one end and tie it with ribbon. Leave the other end open to drop in the gift, hat and joke of your choice. Tie this end and trim the ribbons neatly.

Cut a zigzag edge in the paper at both ends; or leave the ends plain, if you prefer.

Crackers are always a must at the dinner table at Christmas. The diagram above shows the materials required for a cracker: crepe paper for the outside, tissue paper for the lining, and stiff paper and a cardboard cylinder to hold the cracker in shape.

Cut the paper layers as indicated above. Roll them around the tube, and stick them in place securely with either glue or tape. A friction strip can be placed between the stiff paper and cylinder to provide a 'bang' when the cracker is pulled.

Add the final decorative touches — in this case, contrasting layers of crepe paper and a paper motif.

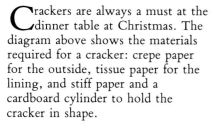

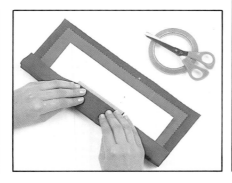

Wire clumps of green amaranthus (love-lies-bleeding) and insert them into the wreath, keeping them generally quite close to the fabric spheres.

Next, wire clumps of white larkspur and intersperse these amongst the amaranthus. These reflect the white in the fabric and add highlights to the arrangement. Wire together several groups of cones and place them standing upright in the arrangement so that they do not get lost among the other plants.

Soften the display by scattering bunches of soft pink rabbit's or hare's tail grass throughout. The seeds tend to moult very easily so be careful when wiring and inserting the grass not to overhandle it.

Pick out the colours in the fabric by dotting clumps of rust coloured nipplewort (or broom bloom) throughout. The dark tones will also add depth to the display.

Finish off with a few colourful satin bows, binding each bow together with wire rather than actually tying it. Insert the bows in amongst the fabric spheres, trailing the tails prettily over the arrangement.

This striking tartan wreath makes a charming centrepiece for the table at Christmas and New Year. First you will need to buy a twig ring from a florist. Begin by individually wiring several heads of red rose. Arrange these in three small groups, evenly spaced around the ring.

Next, wire together nine small bunches of anaphalis (pearl everlasting) and push them into the ring so that they surround the roses. Take three lengths of tartan ribbon and make three single bows, wiring them together rather than actually tying them.

Take a fourth piece of ribbon, fold it in half and push a piece of wire through the folded end: this will form the long 'tails' of the arrangement. Cut a 'V' shape in the ends of the ribbons to finish them neatly, then wire a bow into each of the three gaps between the flowers. To complete the picture, wire the tartan tails beneath one of the bows.

Add several sprigs of holly, again securing them with wire. If the holly is a bit short of berries, you can add some fake berries at this point.

To hang the wreath you will need two lengths of satin ribbon. Each piece should be twice the length of the drop from the ceiling to your hanging height, plus an extra 20cm (8in) for tying around the wreath. Tie each of the four ends opposite one another around the wreath so that the two lengths cross in the centre.

Make four bows from the same colour ribbon and pin them to the wreath over the four tying-on points.

Gently push a length of florist's wire through each of four red wax candles, approximately 1.5cm (½in) above the bases, as shown.

Tthis festive wreath makes an ideal centrepiece if you're short of space on the table — it can be suspended from a hook screwed into the ceiling. Use wire cutters to snip the hook off a coat hanger. Bend the hanger into a circular shape. Bunch damp sphagnum moss around the wire, binding black reel wire or gardener's wire around it to hold it in place.

Take several bushy branches of evergreen, such as cypress, and arrange them to cover the circlet of moss, overlapping the pieces to cover any stalks. Tie the branches to the ring with wire.

Position each candle halfway between two bows, and twist the wire around the wreath to hold it in place. To hang the wreath, tie another length of ribbon around the two main ribbons where they cross, make a loop to go over the hook, and tie the ends in a bow.

A traditional wreath on the front door gives a warm welcome to Christmastime callers. To begin, take a wire coat hanger and pull it into a circle. Bend the hook down to form a loop.

Now wire together small bunches of holly, spruce and other foliage. Then attach each bunch to the circle. Be careful when handling the holly; you can get a bit scratched, and some people can come out in a rash from it. Keep going in one direction until the whole circle is covered.

On top of this add some wired pine cones and, for extra colour, some curly red ribbon. (Use curling gift wrap ribbon for this, running the blunt edge of a pair of scissors along it to make it curl.) Red holly berries look great if you can get hold of them, but they tend to drop very quickly, so they would need replacing often. Finish off with a big red satin bow.

This sort of arrangement always looks very hard to achieve, but in fact it is very simple, provided you assemble everything you need before starting. What you need is a ring of florists' foam with a plastic base, which you can get from a florist. Also buy three plastic candle holders; stick these into the foam.

You will need holly, ivy and fern, all of them either real or fake, plus a selection of dried flowers. Used here are daisy-like sunrays, yellow helichrysum (strawflowers or everlasting), yarrow, safflowers and sea lavender. Simply break pieces off these and stick them into the foam. Try to space the flowers evenly in between the foliage.

When you have finished, stick three candles into the holders already placed. If any of the foliage is real, make sure to keep the foam damp.

IVY CANDLE-RING

FOREST FOLIAGE

This elegant candle-ring is the ideal centrepiece for a festive dinner party but it will only remain fresh for the one occasion. A circular cake base serves as the foundation for the arrangement. Begin by attaching strands of ivy to the edge of the base, securing them with drawing pins.

The sideboard, as well as the table, needs a little dressing up at Christmas. This is bright and cheery, and the materials are quite easy to get hold of. If you don't have woodland nearby your florist should have small sections of bark for sale. Also buy a plastic candle holder. Onto the bark first put a large lump of green Plasticine (modelling clay), and on the top stick your candle holder.

Build up the ring by adding more strands and bunches of leaves until only a small space remains in the centre. Push stems of freesia among the ivy leaves to provide colour contrast.

Now take some plastic or silk fern and spray it gold. Break off pieces when it is dry, and stick them into the Plasticine. Also wire up strands of red paper ribbon, pine cones and red baubles and stick these in.

Use a mixture of white and green candles of varying heights to form the centre of the arrangement. Secure each candle to the base with a blob of glue or Plasticine (modelling clay).

When the Plasticine is artistically concealed, pop a red candle in the holder, and set the arrangement on the sideboard. Put a mat under it, though, or it will scratch the surface.

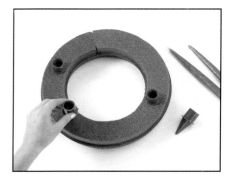

This festive table centrepiece is inexpensive to produce as the foliage used can be found in abundance during the Christmas period. Take a florists' foam ring and insert four candle holders evenly spaced around it.

Dampen the ring and insert four red candles in the holders. We have used hand-made candles for added interest. Now push sprigs of yew into the ring, positioning all the foliage in the same direction.

Next, take four large fir cones and bind wire around the base between the lower scales leaving a long length of wire to insert into the ring. Push the cone wires into the ring between the candles.

Finally, add sprigs of holly and berries to the ring. Berries can be added separately to add colour evenly throughout the decoration. Artificial berries can be used if real ones are not available.

To make this splendid Christmas centrepiece, take a flat circular base such as a cake board and glue a cone of florists' foam to the centre. Then glue or staple a length of gold netting round the edge of the base, gathering it into bunches as you go. Crumple lengths of red fabric or ribbon into double loops and wire the ends. Arrange them in a ring on top of the gold.

Spray a number of Chinese lanterns and lotus seedheads with gold paint. When they are dry, wire the ends and insert them evenly spaced into the cone. Intersperse several long-eared pods throughout, pushing · them deep into the arrangement. Add highlights with a few honesty seedheads (silver dollar plant). Then wire together bunches of small red helichrysum (strawflower or everlasting) and dot them among the other plants, adding colour throughout. Finish off by inserting a few groups of white leaf skeletons — about two to three leaves per group.

Here are two more colourful decorations to hang on the Christmas tree. For the red ball, take a length of cord and wire the ends together, forming a loop. Push the wire right the way through a sphere of florists' foam and double it back on itself — into the foam — to secure. Now cover the foam with flowers.

Pack the flowers tightly into the foam to maintain the spherical shape. Those used here are deep red helichrysum (strawflower or everlasting). Fill in with little clumps of red nipplewort (or broom bloom). To finish, gather up and wire small pieces of silver netting, then insert them amongst the flowers.

This pretty display, arranged in a tiny gift box, makes an attractive miniature decoration. It would also make a delightful present. And with all that lavender, it smells as lovely as it looks. First cut a small block of florists' foam and pop it inside the box. Then wire a couple of red ribbons into bows.

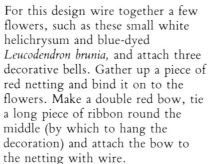

For this design wire together a few flowers, such as these small white helichrysum and blue-dyed *Leucodendron brunia,* and attach three decorative bells. Gather up a piece of red netting and bind it on to the flowers. Make a double red bow, tie a long piece of ribbon round the middle (by which to hang the decoration) and attach the bow to the netting with wire.

Wire together bunches of lavender and pack them into the foam, keeping the arrangement tallest in the middle and splaying it out at the sides. Now scatter tiny, daisy-like glixia or grass daisies throughout; push some deep into the display. Finish off by attaching the two red bows, one to the box, the other higher up on a stem of lavender.

A beautifully wrapped gift is a pleasure to give and a pleasure to receive. So here are over 40 imaginative ways to make your Christmas presents look that extra bit special. Having been shown how to wrap a variety of shapes, you will find some simple ways to make your own wrapping paper — a great cost saver — and lots of pretty decorations such as ribbon ties, rosettes and pom-poms to add those all-important finishing touches. There are also some ingenious ideas for greetings cards that are both simple to make and effective, and, finally, lots of inexpensive ways to make your own gift tags using last year's cards or motifs cut from wrapping paper.

Sometimes the gift wrap seems almost as expensive as the gift itself. But there are plenty of ways to get stylish results without the expense. Reels of gift ribbon can be turned into a vast array of different decorations, from stunning rosettes you couldn't tell apart from shop-bought versions to pretty pom-poms and posies. Braid, cord and even candies can also be used to make gifts that extra bit special.

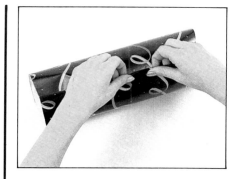

When wrapping a cylinder, avoid using very thick or textured paper as it will be difficult to fold neatly. Cut the paper longer than the cylinder, allowing for extra paper at each end to cover half the cylinder's diameter, and just wider than the gift's circumference. Roll the paper around the parcel and secure with a little tape.

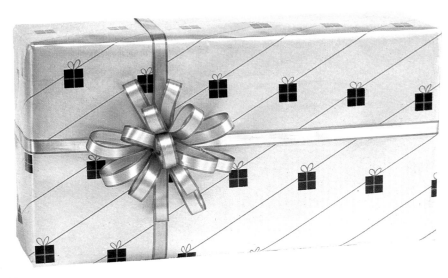

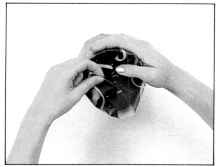

Begin folding the ends of the paper in a series of small triangles as shown here. Continue around the whole circumference, making sure that the 'triangles' are neatly folded into the centre.

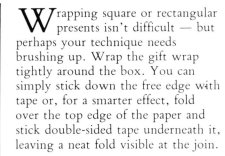

Wrapping square or rectangular presents isn't difficult — but perhaps your technique needs brushing up. Wrap the gift wrap tightly around the box. You can simply stick down the free edge with tape or, for a smarter effect, fold over the top edge of the paper and stick double-sided tape underneath it, leaving a neat fold visible at the join.

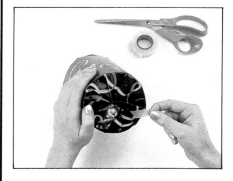

Use a single piece of tape at the centre to fix all the folds in place. If the finished folds are not even, you could cheat a little by sticking a circle of matching gift wrap over each end of the cylinder.

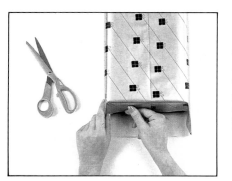

If your paper has a linear design, try to align the design so that the join is not too obvious. Fold the joined section of paper down over the end of the box to make a flap; crease the fold neatly. Trim off any excess paper so there is no unnecessary bulk.

Crease the side flaps firmly, and fold them over the ends of the gift. Smoothing your hand along the side of the box and round on to the end ensures that each flap fits tightly. Fold up the remaining triangular flap, pulling it firmly along the edge of the box, and stick down; use invisible tape (its matt surface is scarcely discernible) or double-sided for the best results.

The usual method of wrapping a sphere is to gather the paper around the gift and bunch it all together at the top. Here is a more stylish method. Put your circular gift in the centre of a square of paper, checking that the two sides of paper just meet at the top when wrapped around the gift. Cut off the corners of the square to form a circle of paper.

Bring one section of the paper to the top of the gift and begin to pleat it to fit the object as shown. The paper pleats at the top of the gift will end up at more or less the same point; hold them in place every three or four pleats with a tiny piece of sticky tape.

Continue pleating neatly and tightly all the way round the circle. It isn't as complicated or as time-consuming as it sounds once you've got the knack! When you have finished, the pile of pleats on top of the gift should look small and neat. Then you can either cover them with a small circle of paper stuck in place or, more attractively, add a bunch of colourful ribbons.

Wrapping awkwardly-shaped presents is just that — awkward. The gift wrap always looks creased and untidy around the angles of the gift. The solution is not to use paper — instead, use brightly-coloured cellophane which doesn't crumple. Cut a square of cellophane a great deal larger than your gift.

Gather the cellophane up and tie it into a bunch above the present. Fan out the excess and add some curled ribbon as a finishing touch. Alternatively, if your gift is cylindrical, roll it in cellophane somewhat longer than the parcel and gather the ends with ribbon.

You will need the type of gift wrap ribbon which sticks to itself when moistened for this decoration. First cut two strips of ribbon at least 40cm (16in) long. Twist each piece into a figure-of-eight, moistening the ends to hold in place. Stick one piece at right angles over the other. Repeat with two more strips 5cm (2in) shorter.

Stick the second rosette on top of the first. To finish, make a loop out of a short strip of ribbon and stick it in the centre. For a more traditional rosette, simply make the loops shorter and tighter.

You can make these decorations in a single colour, but they look more effective if you choose several. For each twist, you need three squares of tissue for the outer colour, two for the middle colour and two for the inner (most visible) section. The squares needed for the inner section are smaller than those for the outside; the middle leaves must be of a size in between.

Pick up the squares in order, putting one on top of the other; outer colour first, then the middle, then the inner squares. Position them so that the corners of each square are at a different angle, as shown. Put a couple of stitches through the centre point to secure all the squares together and leave some thread hanging.

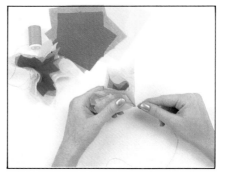

Fold the whole thing in half and half again, twisting the folded point at the base to form the shape of the 'flower'. Pull the thread out at the point, and wind it tightly around the twisted base to secure it; 'fluff' out the finished decoration. Make several 'flowers' and group them together on your present.

CHRISTMAS BOXES

This is a simple but elegant way to use empty gift boxes as containers for pot-pourri. We have selected a green and a black box. Take the lid off one of the boxes and lightly secure three whole flower heads of cow parsley diagonally across it. With aerosol spray paint, give the top of the box two light coats of gold paint.

When the paint is dry, remove the parsley to reveal the unsprayed part of the box. This shows up as a pretty pattern through the paint. Now fix the gold sprayed cow parsley to the other box lid. These boxes are filled with 'Noel' pot-pourri, which is a festive mixture of small cones, tree bark and citrus peel. Cover the pot-pourri with cling film (plastic wrap) before replacing the lids.

POSIES FOR PRESENTS

A delicate posy of dried flowers provides a perfect decoration for any gift. Choose a selection of brightly coloured, small-headed flowers and tie them together with fine wire. The flowers used here are blue larkspur, yellow South African daisy, (a type of helichrysum), small red roses and a touch of golden rod. Wrap a strip of white ribbon around the stems and finish off with a bow.

The posy on this gift box is made up in a similar way, using flowers in a range of colours that match those of the box. The posy contains green amaranthus (love-lies-bleeding), mauve xeranthemums, pink gypsophila (baby's breath), blue larkspur, cream 'cauliflower' and yellow dudinea.

Attach the posies to the gifts with glue. Alternatively you can wire them on. To do this you will need to pierce two small holes in the side of the box. Wrap wire round the stems of the posy and thread it through the holes; secure on the inside.

How to give a tall thin present even more presence! Take a spool of gift ribbon — the sort that sticks to itself when moistened. Roll a length round your thumb to form a small circle; moisten and stick in position.

Make another ring, larger than the first; stick that down too. Make another circle, and another, ensuring that their increase in size is in the same proportion each time. Four circles is about the maximum the ribbon can take before flopping slightly and thus losing the crispness of the decoration.

It is quite easy to paint wide ribbon to co-ordinate with your wrapping paper. And the results are stunning! Choose a gift wrap with a simple design. Decide whether you want the ribbon to be a positive version of the paper's design, like the blue example shown here, or a negative one, like the black and white suggestions. Experiment with poster paint on your chosen ribbon.

Keep the design very simple and stylized. When you're happy with your pattern, paint enough ribbon to wrap up the gift, allowing sufficient for a fairly large bow. Leave the ribbon to dry thoroughly before tying it around the parcel. If the paint does crack a little when tying up the ribbon, simply touch it up and leave it to dry again.

Make a small present look that extra bit special — and that extra bit bigger! Wrap the gift into a ball shape, then cut a strip of paper about three times the width of the gift and long enough to form loops on each side of it. Fold the edges over. Gather small pleats at each end, securing them with sticky tape. Pinch-pleat four gathers in the middle of the strip and secure.

For the trailing sections of the bow, cut a five-sided piece of paper as shown. Fold over the edges in to the centre at the back and secure with tape. Gather pinch pleats at one end and secure. At the other end cut out a V-shaped section to form a nicely-shaped tail. Repeat the procedure a second time.

Turn the pleated ends of the long strip to the middle to form the loops, and secure with double-sided tape. Stick the tails under the bow with more tape. Finally, put double-sided tape over the join on top of the bow and stick the gift in position. Puff out the loops so they look nice and full.

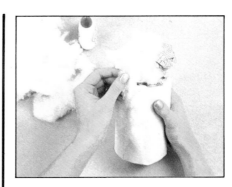

What fun for a child to see Frosty and know that the snowman's hiding a gift! Wrap up a cylindrical gift in paper to form the body of the snowman. Crush newspaper into a shape for the head and stick it on top of the gift. Cover the body with cotton wool (absorbent cotton), sticking it on with dabs of glue. Create a face from bits of paper and stick in place.

For the hat, you need a strip of cardboard, plus a circle big enough to make the brim. Draw an inner circle in the brim, the diameter of Frosty's head; cut it out to form the 'lid' of the hat. Roll the strip of cardboard up to form the crown of the hat; stick it in place with tape.

Stick on the top of the hat, then attach the brim, putting strips of tape inside the crown. Paint the hat with black poster paint; it'll need two or three coats. Wrap around the red ribbon to form a cheery hat-band and put it on Frosty's head. Fray the ends of some patterned ribbon to form a scarf and tie it firmly in place.

With so many presents being exchanged at this time of the year, tags are very important. And they are so easy to make. Draw any festive shape you like on to thin cardboard; this one is a Christmas stocking. Cut out the shape and cover it with bright paper; try to co-ordinate the colours with those in the gift wrap you use for your present.

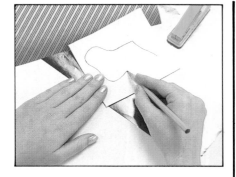

If your wrapping paper has a particular theme in its design make a tag to echo it. To ensure that your design is symmetrical, fold a piece of paper in half and draw on half the design against the fold. Cut around the outline through both layers of paper; open out and use this as a template for the design. Cover a piece of light cardboard with gift wrap and trace around the template.

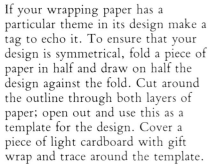

Cut around the outline and punch a hole at the top of the tag. Write your message and tie the tag on to the parcel. You could cheat a little when designing the shape of your tag by tracing an illustration from a magazine or by using the outline of a pastry cutter.

A three-dimensional Santa Claus tag, complete with fluffy beard, provides a jolly festive decoration on a gift. Draw a fairly large rectangle on thin red cardboard; make sure that all the corners are right angles. Score down the middle and fold the cardboard, creasing it well. Draw an inverted 'V' for Santa's hat, and a curve for his chin; cut them out with a craft knife.

Curve the hat and chin outward to give them a three-dimensional look, then draw in the eyes and mouth. Form a beard from a small piece of cotton wool (absorbent cotton), and stick it in position with a dab of glue. Do the same with the fur trim on the edge of the hat and the pom-pom on its tip. Punch a hole in the back of the label, write your message and tie the tag on the parcel.

A heavenly messenger bears the greetings on this Christmas present. Cut a quarter section of a circle from light cardboard to form a narrow cone for the body. On a folded piece of paper draw one arm and one wing against the edge of the fold as shown, so that when they are cut out you will have a pair of each.

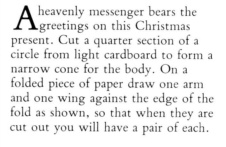

Used greeting cards can often be turned into very acceptable gift tags. Sometimes, as here, the design lends itself to forming a tag. Cut very carefully around the lines of the motif you want to use. Make a hole with a punch, thread a ribbon through the hole and no one would guess the tag had a previous life!

Make the cone and cover it with silver paper (aluminium foil would do). Trace the arm and wings on to silver paper; cut them out and glue them in their relevant positions on the body.

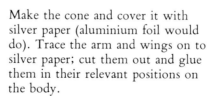

Sometimes a little imagination is needed to give the tag a new and ready-made look. Here, the shape of the tag is outlined on the cardboard in red with a felt-tipped pen. Draw the outline lightly in pencil first to be absolutely sure it is the right size and shape to create the finished label.

Make the head by rolling up some white tissue paper into a firm ball, twisting the ends of the tissue tightly to form a 'neck'. Glue the head into the top of the cone. Tie a scrap of tinsel into a loose knot and stick it on the head as a halo. Make a scroll from white paper, write on your message and stick it between the angel's hands. Attach the angel to the gift with double-side tape.

Colourful puffins, cut from a sheet of wrapping paper, keep a lookout from their perch. Cut a card 28cm x 13cm (18in x 5¼in). The card should be blue on the inside and white on the outside. On the outside, score lines 9cm (3½in) and 19cm (7½in) in from the left and fold. Turn the card over and on the inside score and fold 20cm (8in) in from the left.

Cut out three puffins and spray glue the first one on to the outside of the far right-hand panel of card, facing right. Cut around him with a craft knife leaving him attached to the card by his tail. The score line on the outside will allow him to stand forward.

Glue the other two puffins in place on the inside. Any wrapping paper with a distinct animal motif can be used in this way to make a striking card.

Cut a card 23cm x 18cm (9in x 7in), score and fold in half. Trace the pattern from page 165 and transfer it onto thin cardboard to make a template. Place on some polystyrene wallpaper and draw around it with a soft pencil. Cut out with a craft knife. Also cut out some ice caps and ground from iridescent plastic or silver paper.

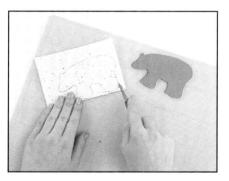

Glue down the mountains, ground and polar bear, placing the latter in front of the peaks. Then decorate with silver sequin stars.

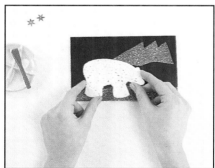

With a silver pen draw in the polar bear's features: the legs, paws and ears. As an alternative, the polar bear could also be made from white felt.

In this section, we demonstrate that a hand-made gift can look both stylish and professional, and be a delight to the recipient. Floral gifts are ideal for female friends and relatives; we have selected a range of ideas to choose from, from pot-pourri bags and picture frames to attractive floral arrangements. For the men in your life, there are desk sets, stationery, photograph frames and modern decorative ornaments, such as the ducks on page 152. We've also included soft toys for the children – or your big sister! – and a number of items which you can enhance by painting: plates, pots and china as well as tea cosies and potato print cushions.

These tiny pot-pourri bags are so easy to create, and they make delightful gifts. Take a length of cotton fabric and, using a plate as a pattern, cut out a circle about 25-30cm (10-12in) in diameter. Hem the edge with running stitch, leaving long tails of thread at either end. Cup the fabric circle in your hand as shown and fill it with pot-pourri.

Gather the fabric into a tight ball by pulling the threads. Secure with a knot. Wire together a small tight bunch of helichrysum (strawflower or everlasting) using fine silver rose wire and attach the posy to the bag, threading the wire through the fabric on both sides to secure. (Use a needle to make holes in the fabric first if necessary.)

Make a double bow out of satin ribbon and wire this on to the bag. finally, cut a length of gold cord about 35cm (15in) long and tie it round the posy, finishing with a double knot. Tie the ends of the cords at the desired length and hang the bag by this loop.

Combine an antique pot with dried flowers for the perfect gift. Note how the blue and orange in the china have been picked up by the colours of the flowers. First, cut a block of florists' foam to fit snugly inside the pot.

Using wired bunches of helichrysum (strawflower or everlasting), build up a dome shape to reflect the shape of the pot. Then add clusters of blue-dyed *Leucodendron brunia*. The unusual bobbly shape of this plant will always add interest to any arrangement.

Finally, add clumps of bright yellow morrison to fill in any gaps and complete the display.

In this attractive design, dried flowers have been used to form a picture. Take a small oval frame and remove the glass, leaving only the backing board. Cut the heads off a colourful selection of plants and start to glue them on to the board. Begin with a red rose in the middle, surrounded by bright yellow yarrow. Add red celosia cockscomb next.

Continue to arrange the heads in small groups, covering the entire surface. The other plants used here are love-in-a-mist heads inside bells of Ireland, lotus seedheads and silver bobbles of *Leucodendron brunia*. The picture is completed with some pearl achillea (a type of yarrow) dotted in amongst the *Leucodendron*.

Drop two or three colours onto the water and swirl together with the end of a paint brush. Cut plain paper to fit the tray. Wearing rubber gloves, start at one end of the tray and lower the paper onto the surface of the water so it can pick up the pattern. Carefully lift up the paper.

Leave the paper to dry overnight on newspaper. You can remove the paint from the tray by drawing strips of newspaper across the surface of the water.

Now you are ready to cover your gift. Cut a rectangle of marbled paper large enough to wrap around the book with a 2.5cm (1in) margin on all sides. Wrap the paper around the book, open the cover and glue the paper inside the opening edges.

Prop up the book so the cover is open at a right angle. Snip the paper each side of the spine and stick the top and bottom margin inside the covers, folding under the corners.

For that extra special gift, cover a plain diary or note book in hand-marbled paper. Fill a shallow tray with water. Put spots of enamel paint on the water with a paint brush. If they sink the paint is too thick and needs thinning with a little white spirit. If they disperse into a faint film it is too thin and should be mixed with more paint.

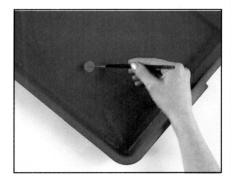

Push the paper at the ends of the spine between the spine and the pages with the points of a pair of scissors. Arrange jewellery stones on the cover and use a strong glue to stick them in place. Cut two pieces of paper to fit inside the covers and glue inside.

Use the traditional art of quilling to make this attractive gift box a gift in itself. Cut coloured paper strips 4mm (³/₁₆in) wide and about 20cm (8in) long. Scratch the end of a strip to soften the paper. Now coil the strip tightly between your thumb and finger. Release the coil so it springs open and glue the end against one side.

The coils can be gently squeezed into various shapes to fit your chosen design. Experiment with forming different shapes such as triangles and teardrops. To make smaller coils, cut shorter paper strips.

Draw a design on the lid of a wooden box and spread paper glue on a section of the lid. Arrange the coils on the glue and then move onto the next section. Fill in the whole design – any gaps around the motif can be filled with coils that match the colour of the box.

Transform ordinary pencils into these smart covered ones with scraps of wrapping paper. Choose round rather than hexagonal-shaped pencils. Cut a strip of wrapping paper wide enough to wrap around the pencil and as long as the pencil. Spray the back heavily with spray glue and wrap around the pencil.

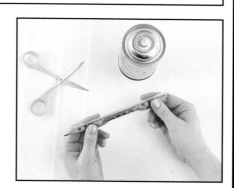

To finish, simply trim away the excess at the end of the pencil with a pair of small scissors.

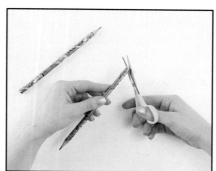

There is no excuse for mislaying letters with this smart letter rack. From thick mounting board cut a rectangle 24cm x 8cm (9½in x 3¼in) for the front and 24cm x 10cm (9½in x 4in) for the back. Diagonally trim away the top corners and cover one side of each piece with giftwrap.

Cut giftwrap slightly smaller than the front and back sections and glue in position on the wrong side. Take a piece of wood 24cm (9½in) long by 3cm (1¼in) wide and 1cm (³⁄₈in) thick. Cover the wood with coloured paper.

Cut a rectangle of mounting board 27cm x 7cm (10½in x 2¾in) for the base and cover with coloured paper. Use a strong glue to stick the front to one narrow edge of the wood keeping the lower edges level. Glue the back to the other side in the same way. Finish the letter rack by gluing this upper section centrally to the base.

Make this carrier bag and you have a gift bag for your presents or go a step further and make the bag itself the present. Cut a piece of thick yellow cardboard 57.5cm x 29cm (22⅝in x 11½in). Refer to the diagram on page 167 and score along the solid and broken lines. Cut away the lower right-hand corner and cut into the base along the solid lines.

Fold the bag forwards along the solid lines and backwards along the broken lines. Turn the bag over and, with a pencil, lightly divide the front into quarters. Cut out a small hole at the centre for the clockwork. Cut out four pieces of red paper 1.5cm x 1cm (⅝in x ³⁄₈in) and glue on the divisions 7cm (2¾in) from the hole.

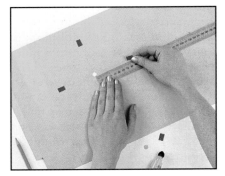

Rub out the pencil lines. Join the side seam by gluing the narrow tab under the opposite end. Fold under the small base sections then glue the long sections underneath. Cut two strips of green cardboard for handles 30cm x 1cm (12in x ³⁄₈in). Glue the ends inside the top of the bag. Insert the clockwork rod through the hole and attach the hands.

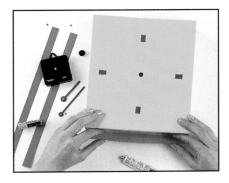

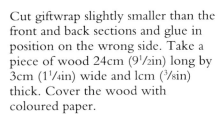

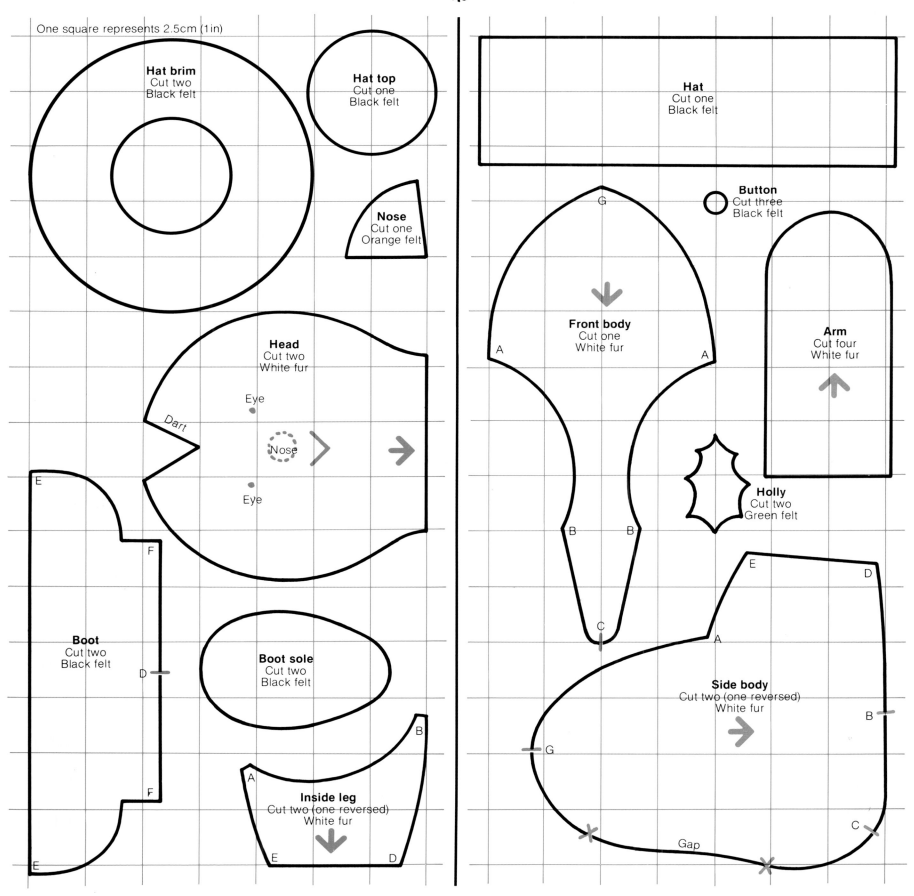

One square represents 2.5cm (1in)

Hat brim
Cut two
Black felt

Hat top
Cut one
Black felt

Hat
Cut one
Black felt

Nose
Cut one
Orange felt

Button
Cut three
Black felt

Head
Cut two
White fur

Eye

Nose

Eye

Dart

Front body
Cut one
White fur

G

A   A

B   B

C

Arm
Cut four
White fur

Holly
Cut two
Green felt

E

F

Boot
Cut two
Black felt

D

F

E

Boot sole
Cut two
Black felt

B

A

Inside leg
Cut two (one reversed)
White fur

E   D

E   D

A

Side body
Cut two (one reversed)
White fur

B

G

C

Gap

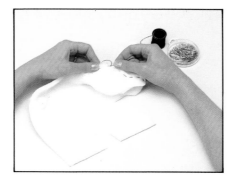

Join the head gusset piece to the side of the head on the side body piece by sewing seam J-K. Repeat on other side. Then sew up seam J-D at the front of the head.

Sew the inside body to the side body, starting at seam D-E. Then sew seam F-G and finally seam H-B. Repeat on other side.

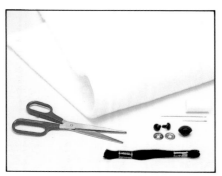

MATERIALS

30cm (12in) white fur fabric
1 pair 13.5mm black safety
  eyes with metal washers
1 small plastic nose
Black embroidery thread
Filling

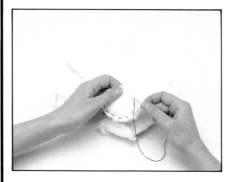

Fold the tail in half lengthwise. Sew along the curved edge, leaving the top open. Turn the tail, poking out the tip carefully. Sew seam K-B on the back of the bear, sewing in the tail at the same time where the two darts meet. Open out and stretch the bottoms of the feet and sew in the foot pads.

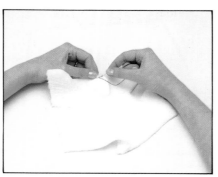

This charming toy will delight any child. Size up the pattern opposite and cut out all the pieces. Pierce a tiny hole at the eye position and cut a slit for the ears on each side body piece. Join both pieces of the inside body by sewing seam A–B, leaving a gap for turning and filling. Open out the inside body. Sew the under chin piece to the inside body along seam C-A-C.

Turn the bear the right way out. Insert the safety eyes through the holes made earlier and secure on the reverse with metal washers. Poke a tiny hole at the very end of the snout and secure the plastic nose in the same way.

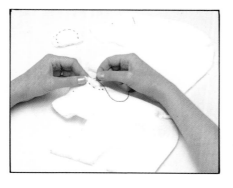

Sew up the darts at the rear of the side body pieces. Sew both halves of ears together, leaving the straight edge open. Turn the right way out and make a small tuck at the raw edge of the ear on both sides to curve the ear slightly inwards and oversew into place. Push the straight edge through the slit in the side body and sew the ears into position through all layers of fabric.

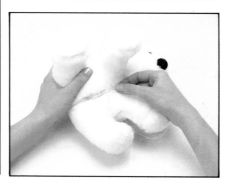

Fill the bear with stuffing, starting at the feet. Flatten the feet slightly as the filling is added. Mould the head shape by pushing more filling into the cheeks. When satisfied with the general shape of the bear, close the gap in the tummy using a ladder stitch.

With black embroidery thread, stitch through the feet four times on each paw to form claws. Using the same thread, embroider a smile on the bear's face. Finish off the mouth on either side with a small stitch at right angles to the main stitch.

Finally, taking a long needle and white thread, pull the eyes slightly together by passing the threaded needle from corner to corner of the opposite eyes, through the head. Fasten off securely.

One square represents 2.5cm (1in)

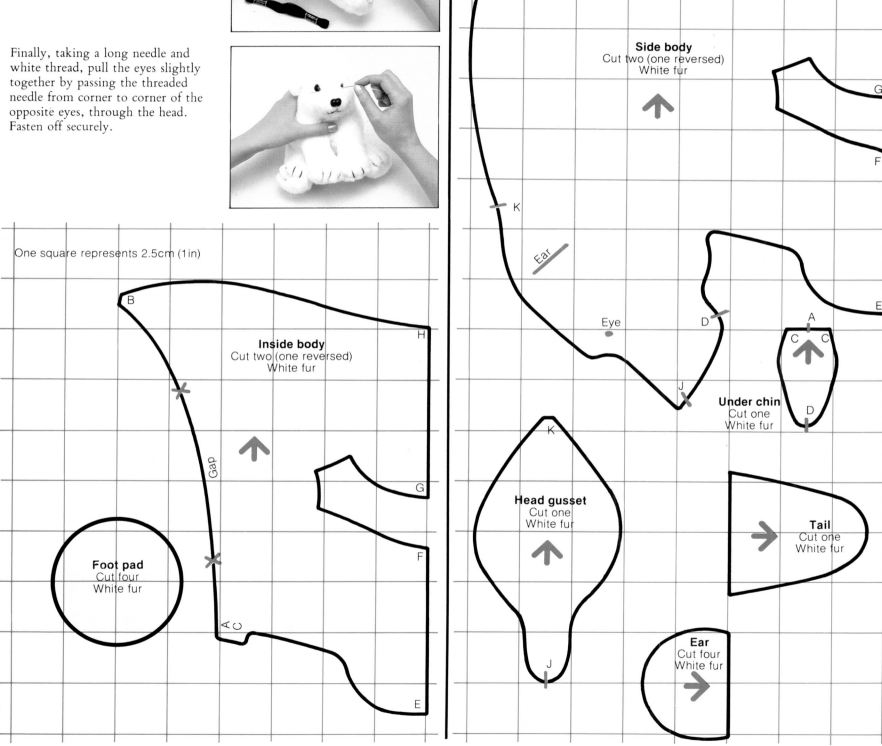

Side body
Cut two (one reversed)
White fur

Dart

Tail

B

G

F

K

Ear

Eye

D

A

C C

J

Under chin
Cut one
White fur

D

B

Inside body
Cut two (one reversed)
White fur

H

Gap

G

F

A
C

E

Foot pad
Cut four
White fur

K

Head gusset
Cut one
White fur

J

Tail
Cut one
White fur

Ear
Cut four
White fur

Size up the templates on the following pages as follows: draw up a grid of 2.5cm (1in) squares, then copy the design onto your grid, square by square, using the grid lines as a guide.

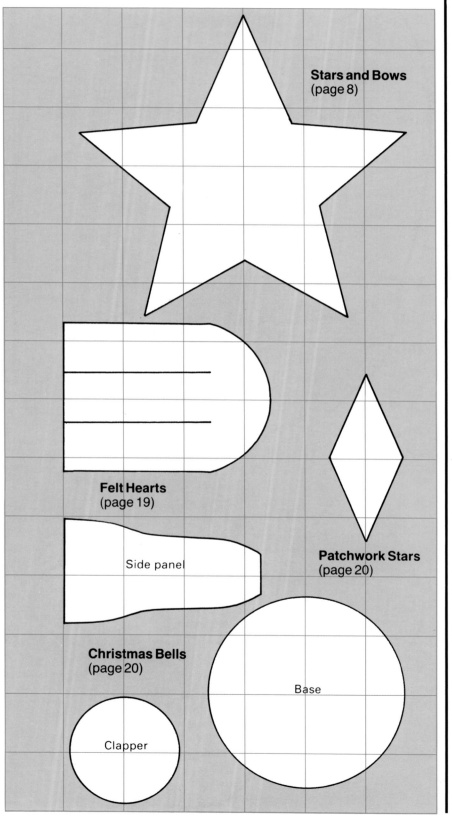

Stars and Bows
(page 8)

Felt Hearts
(page 19)

Side panel

Patchwork Stars
(page 20)

Christmas Bells
(page 20)

Clapper

Base

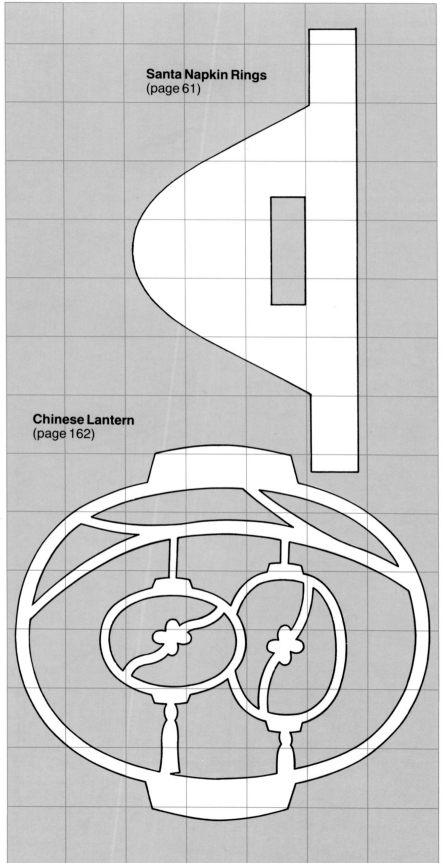

Santa Napkin Rings
(page 61)

Chinese Lantern
(page 162)